# THINGS WE SAID TODAY

Other Stride anthologies:

*A Curious Architecture: a selection of contemporary prose poems*
edited by David Miller and Rupert Loydell

*The Rainbow's Quivering Tongue: an anthology of women's poetry*
edited by Mary Plain

*How The Net Is Gripped: a selection of contemporary American Poetry*
edited by David Miller and Rupert Loydell

*The Stumbling Dance*
edited by Rupert M. Loydell

*Jewels & Binoculars: fifty poets celebrate Bob Dylan*
edited by Phil Bowen

*Completing The Picture: exiles, outsiders & independents*
edited by William Oxley

*Stonechat: ten Devon poets*
edited by Christopher Southgate

*Ladder To The Next Floor: Stride Magazine 1-33*
edited by Rupert M. Loydell (University of Salzburg Press)

# THINGS WE SAID TODAY

*edited by*
**Phil Bowen**

THINGS WE SAID TODAY
First edition 1995
Selection © Phil Bowen
Poems © individual authors

ISBN 1 873012 78 0

Cover design Joe Pieczenko
Cover concept by Phil Bowen

Acknowledgements
'New York City Blues' by Adrian Henri
is reprinted from *Penny Arcade* (Jonathan Cape).
'No Teenage Crime' is reprinted from *Flesh Or Money* (Littlewood).
'Beatles' by Adrian Mitchell first appeared in *The Listener*.
'Variation On A Lennon And McCartney Song' by Wendy Cope
is reprinted from *Serious Concerns* (Faber).
'Captain Of The 1964 Top Of The Form Team' and 'Liverpool Echo'
by Carol Ann Duffy are reprinted from *Mean Time*
and *Standing Female Nude* (Anvil Press).
'Annus Mirabilis' by Philip Larkin is reprinted from *High Windows*
by permission of Faber and Faber.
From 'A Letter To Tom Horton' by Stuart Sutcliffe
is taken from *Backbeat* by Pauline Sutcliffe and Alan Clayson
and is reprinted by permission of Pauline Sutcliffe.
'Conversation On A Train' by Roger McGough
is reprinted from *In The Glass Room* (Cape)
by permission of Peters, Fraser and Dunlop.

Published by
Stride Publications
11 Sylvan Road, Exeter
Devon EX4 6EW
England

# CONTENTS

## EDITORIAL

I first heard 'Love Me Do' on my thirteenth birthday in October 1962 at the Youth Club my Uncle Doug ran at St. Stephen's Church, Wavertree, in Liverpool. I asked my cousin David who the record was by; he not only knew, but had actually seen one of the group, John Lennon, at a bus stop in Woolton.

Soon afterwards I saw the Beatles myself. It was their first television appearance on a programme called 'People and Places', and immediately realised that I had seen them before.

Curiously, it was in the shop window of Albert Marrion's, a wedding photographer opposite the Penny Lane roundabout, near where I lived. What stays in my mind most however, is not so much the surly Beat group in their black leather, so out of place amongst the brides and grooms, but the fact that I first saw the Beatles at – of all places – Penny Lane. And before they made it big.

*Phil Bowen* May 1995

Special thanks to Ann Gray for popping up with the title, and to Damian Furniss for checking one or two things out. A very special thanks to all the poets who made the book possible

'You have to be a real sour square not to love the nutty, noisy, handsome Beatles.'

*Daily Mirror* editorial, November 1963

## from ANNUS MIRABILIS

Sexual intercourse began
In nineteen sixty-three
(Which was rather late for me) –
Between the end of the *Chatterley* ban
And the Beatles' first LP.

Up till then there'd only been
A sort of bargaining,
A wrangle for a ring,
A shame that started at sixteen
And spread to everything.

Then all at once the quarrel sank:
Everyone felt the same,
And every life became
A brilliant breaking of the bank,
A quite unlosable game...

*Philip Larkin*

## ALPHABEATLES

A is for the AMPS
that couldn't compete
with the shrieking hordes
that drowned out the beat.

B's for the BEAUTY
that no-one foresaw
could come from four scruffs
from a northern shore.

C's for the CAVERN
where Brian Epstein
found the local stars
were starting to shine.

D's for the DRUM-
kit that Ringo hit
like your funny-bone
with his dry Scouse wit.

E is for EARS that
were covered in hair
yet of great music
wrote more than their share.

F is for FAME
'greater than Jesus':
a statement that gave
the God-squad seizures.

G is for GEORGE whose
shy ways struck a chord
with ladies who screamed
out for their sweet lord.

H is for HAMBURG,
a grim German port,
where marks weren't many
and the gigs weren't short.

I's for IMAGINE
that some mixed-up kid
would gun down John Lennon.
None of us did.

J's for the JOINT
Bob Dylan got going:
Suck on this wind
where the answer's blowing.

K's the KALEIDOSCOPE
eyes of the girls
the Cynths and Jackies
and Chrissies and Shirls.

L is for the LOVE
that is all you need.
For a moment it seemed
the world agreed.

M's the MERSEY,
that great shining current
they all four had
as a common parent.

N is for the NIGHT
that was A Hard Day's:
lasting monument
to a passing craze.

And O's for OH BOY!
have you heard the news?
Paul must be dead
'cause he's not wearing shoes.

P's for PRODUCER,
the great George Martin,
who opened the door
and let some art in.

Q's for QUEEN LIZ
who awarded them gongs
for invading the States
with groovy songs.

R's for REVOLVER,
a radical disc
you could live without,
but why take the risk?

And S for SHIRELLES,
young, gifted and black.
Liverpool, Africa,
New World and back.

T's for TIES skinny,
toes pointy and tab-
collared shirts you had
to wear to be fab.

U's for the UNITY
coming apart
as the decade wore out
and broke its heart.

V's for the VAST
sums of money they made
proving juvenile style
a worldwide trade.

W's the WIRRAL,
those church-hall gigs:
birds in vans, local fans,
cheap scent and cigs.

X the ingredient
ninety per cent
of rival bands
couldn't seem to invent.

Y is for YELLOW,
their submarine's hue,
which means that this poem
is nearly through.

but for Z, the ZEBRA
crossing they strode
out of our lives on
across *Abbey Road*.

John Gibbens

## from **A LETTER TO KEN HORTON**

…washed out with talk, sick of faces, fed up of cathedrals and squares, tired of sitting all day, tired of black and white furniture, tired of seeing so many people jabbering away about nothing. Liverpool! Meaning the Cracke, the Jacaranda, the college, the flat,
NDD, tired of 'egg on toast and a tea, please'.

In that Liverpool I know not one thing stands out in my memory. The city sprouts like a huge organism, diseased in every part, the beautiful thoroughfares only a little less repulsive because they have been drained of their pus. Liverpool. When I have something to give, I will give it. When I have something to say, I will say it in paint, in stone or anything my soul touches…

*Stuart Sutcliffe*

## PILS AND SPEED

*'At that point... they didn't even sound like The Beatles. They were a raw, amphetamine- and beer-driven. They were an early version of a punk band.'* – Ringo Starr.

Before moptop heads sprouted a craze of hair
and grey suits were shredded for kaftans and furs.
Before 'Scrambled Eggs' became 'Yesterday'
and the folk in the posh seats rattled their jewels.

Before grannies hummed their hits through gummy mouths
and kids beat time on the grills of radiograms.
Before the manic panic of wet knickered girls
falling faint in the arms of the great British Bobby.

Before Molly met Des. Before George met Patti.
Before he and God blundered into wife swapping.
Before Paul died, was buried and rose again
and vinyl effigies burned across the southern states.

Before the Yogi Mahareshi unbuttoned his fly
and the shotgun composers got a quickie divorce.
Before the periscope of the Yellow Submarine
spied an Oriental Harpy with the naked walrus.

Before Zimmerman misheard 'I wanna hold your hand'
and turned our boys on to all-American grass.
Before Doctor Robert dropped his first sugar lump
and the cold turkey flapped its featherless stumps.

Before Sgt. Pepper got his friends together
and dressed them up in silks and braids.
Before the audition was passed and Apple Corp
gave away more money than it made.

Before Stu blew a fuse and his light went black
and Pete won the best lookin' poll and got the sack.
Before Rory's storm died and Ringo switched kits.
Before Brian cruised the Cavern and was smitten.

And a few years after Long John Silver
donned a boot lace tie and drainpipe jeans
and busked Lonnie skiffle with the Quarry Men
at the Woolton church fete jamboree

Five unlikely lads stomped holes in the stage
of a harbour strip joint for twenty quid a week.
Hired by gangsters, watched by sailors and whores
set on bawling and brawling; getting baited

By our boys in jackboots and swastika'd caps,
their hollers copied from the yankee pioneers
at the wild frontier of rhythm and blues; hip cats
rocking a bar-room beat; their drums and guitars

Fuelled by purple hearts and frothy beer,
enough to raise a sweat in the black leather kecks
of red blooded scousers after fame and sex;
kicking the sixties into first gear

By pulling fräuleins – catching 'Hamburg Throat' –
burning down the house: deported by boat
back to the sweat-caves of the Liverpool scene
to make those records; to live those dreams.

*Damian Furniss*

## THIRTEEN IN SIXTY-THREE

We were all thirteen in sixty-three.
Profumo and a Russian spy sharing the same Marylebone mews.
After Love Me Do came Please Please Me.

From Me To You soon to be M.B.E.
Supermac in the mask? Christine Keeler in the news.
We were all thirteen in sixty-three.

Staying up late with T.W.3.
Stephen Ward picking up the tab – the Establishment's dues.
After Love Me Do came Please Please Me.

Harold Wilson's white heat of technology,
The fourteenth Earl of Home on the grousemoor in his trews.
We were all thirteen in sixty-three.

Jack Kennedy's Promised Land across the sea
From an island full of noises; John Lennon had lit the fuse.
After Love Me Do came Please Please Me.

The Shrimp's dress four inches above the knee!
A few of the great train robbers on the boat to Santa Cruz.
We were all thirteen in sixty-three.
After Love Me Do came Please Please Me.

*Phil Bowen*

# POET NOT PROFIT

*(a true tale in failed Skeltonics)*

Just at the time
I was learning to rhyme
It fell to my youthful lot
Not to talent spot
But organise a dance.
Which is to say that once
For a students' society
Of which I was secretary
I had to hire a band,
For the usual cash-in-hand.
It was the nifty 'Fifties then
Of Suez and Macmillan
That ran into the 'Sixties when
Students were of use
And could afford to pick and choose.
And I, not Stephen, was pretender
To being the last and biggest spender,
So when offered four lads of Liverpool
Proved the biggest fool:
And though they only wanted forty quid
Hired another band (I did!),
Preferring for two hundred smackers then
Kenny Ball and his Jazzmen.
But within a hundred days
I knew the error of my ways,
For the Beatles shot to fame
And I to fellow student blame.
But at least I learned a lesson then:
Poets are not businessmen
And cannot ever make a profit
Nor turn prophet for a buck,
But only hope, with a little luck,
Never for a rhyme to be stuck,
Nor descend to prose or worse
And have to give up writing verse.

*William Oxley*

# ROCK'N'ROLL BOOGIE-WOOGIE BLUES

I was a spotfaced kid about fourteen years at school
Spent my time drawing cartoon pictures and playing the fool
I watched *People & Places* saw four pretty faces
Singing 'bout Love Me Do.
Switched the TV off – they'd done enough
I said 'that's how I feel too.'
My daddy bought me a new guitar and I looked in the mirror
Singing : 'Dig these rhythm'n'blues.'

I studied painting at the college, blew my diploma too
My momma and my poppa sayin' 'Son what you gonna do?'
I saw a sign in the sky and a real cool guy
Told me I got nothing to lose
So I picked up my guitar and I looked in the mirror
Singing: 'Dig these rhythm'n'blues.'

It's alright
I'm feeling confused
It's alright
I got the rock'n'roll star boogie-woogie blues

Like a reincarnation of Johnny B. Goode
I make a funky boogie-woogie like a boogie-woogie should
With the cats in the band rockin' right behind
We believed we could change all the laws this time
So I plugged in my guitar and I looked at the people
Singing dig these rhythm'n'blues

It's alright
I'm feeling confused
It's alright
I got the rock'n'roll star
Faded painter
Jaded teacher
Clapped out writers
Facing up to fact-u-ality
Boogie woogie blues

*John Cornelius*

## THE DAY OUR BUDGIE DIED

I'm barely done with launching off
the worn red moquette arm of our settee
(sofas, on our estate, somewhat affected)
and screaming FIREBALL XL5, when Mum,
too distraught to reinforce rules,
announces poor Willoughby's demise...

I cry the length of an impossibly quiet road
to a name-escapes-me friend's house, and we
are out the back, tittling dolls on their toes –
maybe we don't speak because she won't play rockets –
but difficult joint-sulk over, she is
worryingly remote, singing Love-love-me do

whilst the big brother, who's helped the
Not-Yet-Fab ones afford the cost of
four pretty risky haircuts, lifts
for the fifth or sixth time,
the cream plastic arm
of his suitcase-sized portable, and
outlining future grooviness,
I know I know that tune...

*Sandra Tappenden*

# HISTORY

*for Michelle*

She was through with Pythagoras,
had screwed up any chance
of pursuing Maths to 'O' level,
college or university. Couldn't do
with the persistent hassle
of revision eight days a week.

Yesterday scratched with crossed nibs,
whispered in *The Mayor of Casterbridge*,
quivered with rabbits' reproductive organs.
Experiments with pan-stick and kohl
were measured by cat-calls from the lads.

Her head was a laquered beehive,
a cavern full of woodworm that emerged
as Beatles. Petticoats and Jive were out –
a shift through Twist to Rock'n'Roll.
Orange satin stretched across her hips,
creased and wrinkled at the waist,

flapped awkwardly about her bust;
wrecked – among the windfalls –
by the horny hands of a dairyman
at the Young Farmers' annual hop,
as John, Paul, George and Ringo
swung past, with a band of nowhere men,
breathing beer and cigarettes, screaming
*Please Please Me* and *You Can't Do That.*

She hung on to her virginity,
scraped through English and Biology –
got an 'A' for Art; put Pythagoras
and the ruined dress down to history.

*Miriam Obrey*

## THERE'S A PLACE

11/6 from NEMS. The 'Twist and Shout' E.P.
And all I had to do was say thanks Dad,
still in his drab raincoat and trilby,
and before my mothers started brightening up

the backyard, whitewashing walls, fastening trellises,
and planting flowers in anything they'd grow in.
I was home early. He was on shifts: 'There's something
from your father in the front room.'

That first L.P.! Pulling those four grins out of the paper bag,
Ringo still with his quiff, I'd mime: 'One two three four...'
in front of the new three-piece suite. They could see me
in the house opposite since my mother had chopped down the hedge.

And Dad, a detective waking up in the driving seat,
Liverpool, a gaberdine terrace of schooldays,
glad hairstyles were changing; hope for this boy
who could never achieve a quiff that would stay.

Now he tells me he went along 'with what your mother wanted,'
these last few years like squints from a fortune teller's ball:
moving house   a favourite area   I can see a beautiful garden,
but over here   something cloudy   unexpected   bad.

Despite the news about his sight on top of everything else,
he carries on, makes the best of it, allowing nature
and the way weather can change, to work things out,
looks older, and for company, crossing the road in a cap.

The music-centre's a godsend. It's usually the sixties you can hear
now the phone's in the lounge, now he can't clearly make out a face
And someone else does the garden the way she'd have liked it,
and last night,   familiar background voices:

>     'The...ee...ee...ere. There's a place...'

*Phil Bowen*

## NOT A SECOND TIME

Friday. Double Physics. Miss Longbottom.
Behind the hiss of burners they were
whispering. Someone thought I ought to know.

My boyfriend and Pat Spring snogged all night
queuing for the Beatles. They were down beside
the Regal. My father wouldn't let me go.

I had tears like razors in my throat,
sweating palms, when I snapped the ruler
straight across the heart, right through
Ann loves Keith. Keith loves Ann.

After school he gave me the tickets,
told me it meant nothing, not to him.
All through the screaming and the music

I saw Pat Spring's gloating smile.
Keith sang along with All My Loving.
I cried with Not A Second Time.

No, no, n,n,n,n,no, not a second time.

*Ann Gray*

**'NO TEENAGE CRIME WAS RECORDED
DURING THE BEATLES APPEARANCE
ON THE ED SULLIVAN SHOW IN 1964,
IN THE U.S.A.'**

We're all home
no more liqor store
    watching
the Beatles
    in 1964.

Sheath that shiv
punks against the law
    cruising
the airwaves
    in 1964.

Spook the rich
finger-lickin' poor
    filching
the hand-outs
    in 1964.

Jo loves John
read it on the shore
    surfing
the white caps
    in 1964.

Daddy-o
caught us in the raw
    pulling
our plonkers
    in 1964.

I love you
roll me on the floor
    getting
a feel up
    in 1964.

John Paul George
Ringo out to score
      goosing
the groupies
      in 1964.

Uncle Sam
soon we're off to war
      dreaming
of Vietnam
      in 1964.

Rip it up!
Man, this *is* a bore
      watching
the Beatles
      in 1964.

*Wes Magee*

## SHE LOVES YOU AT ELK HORN

Two years on from news film of Russian missiles
heading for Castro's Cuba before getting to me,
The Beatles' *She Loves You* invaded Iowa's
small-town homes like subversive messages by Krushchev
on our deluxe black and white TVs.

1964, and living was in the balance of fear, violence and
a love the Beatles were about to bring: throwing a pitchfork
at my friend as he ran to a dark shed left four red holes
in his invisible head (and missing the eyes
was an act of the god I believed in then).

Elk Horn's one school still drilled
air-raid practices under old wooden desks with a terrified
face between your knees and time for quick dreams:
nuclear death, or English haircuts to shake on
*Yeah, Yeah, Yeah* and drive all the girls to screams.

When we watched those Fab Four on the Ed Sullivan Show
we were beginning to learn about the surprise of change.
All you had to do was be there to listen
and it was like absorbing the same instant of shock
that rocked when Clay stole the history of Liston.

They startled in their clean-cuts suits and ties –
those harmonies as pure as Country and Western or hymns!
It was like a sudden revolution from within
and the airwaves would whirl like a Midwestern tornado
to scythe fields of corn or raise churches to the floor.

It was much later when I rode on the magical tour,
chased after diamonds and that mystery
sown in the multi-coloured clouds of adolescent skies
by John, Paul, George, Ringo and Lucy.
Here was just one future hinted to a ten year old's eyes.

*Mike Ferguson*

## THE CLOSEST THING TO PRAYER.../
## SATURDAY NIGHT AND SUNDAY MORNING

some nights disgorging from Dance-Halls and
street-corner drifting from dockside pubs
we take motor metallic-screaming bikes down
roads crystal-clear with amber lighting,
then overlooking the moon-crazy estuary
spidered with shipyard cranes and derricks,
past Salt End jetties and chemical plants
to the all-night Café where 'Twist and Shout'
and 'She Loves You' strike the air dumb,
vibrating the huge Wurlitzer jukebox and
pinball tables lit up like neon hoardings

drink acrid expresso coffee in Duralex cups
to kill alcohol swirling around the brain,
watching Honda and BSA in formation beneath
the arc of street light. Talking trash

then drunk and chasing midnight girls
we pause to see the distant lights of
trawlers throb across the estuary stillness,
off for Iceland or Baltic fishing grounds

and we pause
for a moment
to watch

*Andy Darlington*

## FOR RACHEL

I always pleaded with her
To put on our special record,
*She loves you, yeah, yeah, yeah,*
It soothed me back
Into our casual routine
After my stormy weekends away.

She wasn't easy to live with.
Eccentricity coloured all her motives,
Which I would wait to backfire onto me.
But I loved her
For her lack of conformity
And her Beatles records.

Friday nights were frightening with her.
To fit everything in
Including a 3 a.m. swim
In the black Morecombe sea.
I usually left early,
Then laid awake til 4,
Heard her key
Hoping she'd come home alone,
Snuggle up with me
In those musty smelling quilts
We'd salvaged from the skip along the street,
When they'd modernised the Hacienda Hotel.

Sometimes she'd come in loudly –
A man she'd picked up,
(Three guesses he worked at
Heysham Power Station
And was called John)

And then she died.
A chicken pox virus.
I hadn't known she was a Christian
And wasn't that lucky as she'd go to heaven.
I cried because I wasn't one then

And not allowed to play
*Ticket to Ride* at her funeral.

Later we knackered the jukebox at the pub,
Their only Beatles tune,
Drinking stiff upper lip shorts,
Until the regulars complained we were morbid,
Interfering with their pints
And got thrown out.

Still we sang *From Me To You*
Along the towpath all the way home.
I got the record though,
The same scratch through.

*Lesley Marshall*

## THINGS WE SAID TODAY

Worcester Park 1965

How that latch on the gate
still jams at Number One
Hundred and Seventeen
Langley Avenue: it gets
right to you. 'Me, I'm just
a lucky kind...' peters
to guitar when you turn
the chipped handle. In.

Smeared by decades
of treatment
– that lotion glazed
from crowns settling
down for *Peyton Place* –
those antimacassars
are still going. Ever so
slightly they might glint
if the afternoon sun
rounds on their oiliness
at the right angle.
You check underneath:

a sudden rectangle
of the original
pattern stuns: some Eden
for an endless Paisley
is there in its glory
of garish fibre. Why
were heads never allowed
further than the yellowed
protectors? French windows
rattle but hold away
that breeze to cool sitters.
The covered-over room
starts to its thousand sounds:
'Elbows off the table,
young Pete.' You hear, Still there

clenched, vertical, your
expectant knife and fork
over ridges of a linen
blue-squared tablecloth
or a tray rafia-edged.
That tea in your cup scums
itself some protection:
the air, you reflect, must
have awful things in it.
You find yourself humming
'Things We Said Today' and
cannot find the right words.
You see the characters.
Windows boil over. 'Two Way
Family Favourites'
makes its requests quite clear:
you find your own number
distinct from all those stars.
Cilla, Dusty, The Kinks
tangle with hot lamb fat
as you are taken up
a raked gravel drive.
Here, Uncle Bob, vest on,
does interminable
clever things with leads
and screwdrivers under
a *Corsair* bonnet.
Hairy-backed, Player's
in cheeky mouth, he takes
a drag and exhales words
through nostrils: 'Someday when
we're dreaming...' Ignition

and he starts to re-live
the game at Stamford Bridge
with its last gasp winner.
('Smell that cauliflower!')
The idling speed's all wrong:
he adjusts the timing.
'You're certain it's not that
carburettor playing up.

Just turn it over for us
would you, Pete?'
We all wait.

                    *Peter Carpenter*

# THE CAPTAIN OF THE 1964 *TOP OF THE FORM* TEAM

*Do Wah Diddy Diddy, Baby Love, Oh Pretty Woman,*
were in the Top Ten that month, October, and the Beatles
were everywhere else. I can give you the B-side
of the Supremes one. Hang on. *Come See About Me?*
I lived in a kind of fizzing hope. Gargling
with Vimto. The clever smell of my satchel. Convent girls.
I pulled my hair forward with a steel comb that I blew
like Mick, my lips numb as a two-hour snog.

No snags. The Nile rises in April. Blue and White.
The humming-bird's song is made by its wings, which beat
so fast that they blur in flight. I knew the capitals,
the Kings and Queens, the dates. In class, the white sleeve
of my shirt saluted again and again. *Sir!... Correct.*
Later, I whooped at the side of my bike, a cowboy,
mounted it running in one jump. I sped down Dyke Hill,
no hands, famous, learning, *dominus domine dominum.*

*Dave Dee Dozy...* Try me. Come on. My mother kept my mascot
    Gonk
on the TV set for a year. And the photograph. I look
so brainy you'd think I'd just had a bath. The blazer.
The badge. The tie. The first chord of *A Hard Day's Night*
loud in my head. I ran to the Spinney in my prize shoes,
up Churchill Way, up Nelson Drive, over pink pavements
that girls chalked on, in a blue evening; and I stamped
the pawprints of badgers and skunks in the mud. My country.

I want it back. The captain. The one with all the answers. *Bzz.*
My name was in red on Lucille Green's jotter. I smiled
as wide as a child who went missing on the way home
from school. The keeny. I say to my stale wife
*Six hits by Dusty Springfield.* I say to my boss *A pint!*
*How can we know the dancer from the dance?* Nobody.
My thick kids wince. *Name the Prime Minister of Rhodesia.*
My country. *How many florins in a pound?*

    *Carol Ann Duffy*

## RINGO HATED ONIONS

rumours for weeks
would it be the Palais or the Odeon
and how to get the time
off school to queue for tickets

a foggy Saturday
the whole town snaking
round the block and back again
frost pinching our thighs
us huddled in our PVC macs

do you think we stand a chance
do you know Ringo hates onions
Shirley points to a piece
on today's front page that says
they all love Jelly Babies

we take plenty
Janice bites the heads off
as we pelt the Fab Four
and Ringo catches one of mine

he grins right back at me
shakes his hair the way he does
love me do
this is the night

Sandra screams so much
she wets her knickers
Brenda Cunliffe gets carried away
by St John's Ambulance

but I keep my head
first to the stage door
strong against the push and press
he's expecting me
I wanna hold your hand

he winks
asks my name and writes it
with love from me to you
across his photo in the programme

we'll drink scotch and coke
I'll be introduced
to Paul, John and George
it's going like a dream
I haven't eaten onions for weeks

*Pamela Johnson*

# HARD DAY'S NIGHT

John, Paul, George
and Ringo lived
amongst Aunt Grace's
butterfly collection

John the scarab imagining
new skies for his rolling sun
Paul every-where-man cockroach
wings barely folded
George's blue-green carapace
like petrol in puddles ·
and Ringo off his pin
among fallen scales

Aunty Grace took me
for A Hard Day's Night
I wanted Disney

how could the fab four let
my Grandad cut their hair
like German Helmets
like mine

and where was the story
why such silly suits
stiff as crimplene frocks
Nan sewed for Sindy

that night John, Paul, George
and Ringo scuttled from skirting boards
swarmed with their fans
over the kitchen floor

fleeing my torch beam
as I stamped
and stamped
and stamped

*Llinora Milner*

## AUTOGRAPHS

I went to Paul's house in Forthlin Road
off ours but at the council end
for his autograph

   and left my book there (because he wasn't home)
   and when I went for it his dad let me in
      to see which book was mine
   and he asked me if Paul had signed it
   and he had
   and his brother was there
   and wasn't he in the Scaffold?
   and I could hear girls giggling outside
   and they were peering in through the nets
   and now they run coach parties to look at the house
   but nobody lets them in
      (I suppose they've moved away – I would)
   and years later, I offered the autograph
      to a girl I'd really fancied for ages
   and she took it
   but she didn't want me

I still have
   Max Jaffa
   Cardinal Heenan
   and two of Gerry and the Pacemakers

*Michael Cunningham*

# BUT WHAT HAPPENED TO PETE BEST?

He must have gone somewhere.
What does he do with his days? Does he sit
low and lonely long hours in some Huyton pub
where everyone avoids his eyes?

Bad luck has a smell about it. After a while
people stay out of your way. Success
is different, smells good, smells of money,
power, sex, fast cars and perfume.

Gerry Marsden, he bought a butcher's shop
and took to boning carcasses, until the old urge
got too strong. Went back on the road,
gigs at the tinsel halls, Torquay, Southport.

But what happened to Pete Best?
Was there a band somewhere
needed a drummer with a steady kick,
no frills, get on with the business;

or was there a career in double-glazing,
biscuits, unit trusts? A long road down,
door after door, waiting for sales to come;
after that, the Kleeneeze man.

I wonder if Paul ever sends him postcards?
Maybe George asks him round once in a while,
they sit out on the sun terrace with long drinks
and avoid talking about music, or first wives.

I bet he never called his son Zak,
I bet his kids never went to Millfield.
I bet he's sitting there, right now, reading this poem
in a comfortable chair, with his wife cooking dinner

and the Sunday sun high over Birkenhead.
I bet he's thickened round the waist, contented
and drawing a five figure salary. I bet he laughs
when he thinks of the old days. I bet he doesn't.

Hamburg: a bunch of kids who spoke no German
in Scouse accents yet to become fashionable;
three-chorders, often out of tune – the rude forefathers
of garage grunge, thrashing rock standards for the troops.

And now look at them: dead famous everywhere,
dead wealthy, dead involved with health foods and charities,
dead incapable of cutting good songs any more. Dead disappointed,
Pete, that it didn't turn out differently. Look at Stuart and John.

Fame is a strange mistress. John was so famous that he had to die,
Paul is so famous that everyone writes him begging letters,
George is so famous that I don't know where he is,
Ringo's so famous that everyone wants to have a drink with him.

And Pete's famous for not making it,
famous for not being famous, the nearly man,
the one who was only ordinary after all.
From this business, Pete, no-one gets out alive.

*Tony Charles*

## LIZZY IN THE SKY WITH DIAMONDS

My dad says he was the drummer
who left The Beatles.
I told all my friends,
hugged my pillow excitedly at night.

On my stage of splintered pallets
I was Sergeant Pepper's Lonely Hearts Club band;
running on rusty oil drums for Mr Kite,
the Hendersons a riff raff of tabby cats,

dreaming of Dad behind me I sang
'Love Me Do' and 'Please Please Me',
pasting the sergeant's cardboard moustache
onto my plastic doll.

Now, I don't care that dad scraped washboards,
not snares – never sang 'Penny Lane',
but 'Sailing', arms, like canvas,
waving into the Yorkshire wind.

*Lizzy Lister*

## GOT TA GET YOU INTA MY LIFE

He was always known as the Dark Horse, and some people
say he's awkward or earnest or even haunted
but to me he always looks like George.

She looked a bit like Pattie Boyd, long and blonde
and what you'd call bewitching, and she was giddy
over him, too; after all those years there she stood
sipping spring water and throwing spells.

The way he comes sliding down them notes in Nowhere Man
is sacred and on Inner Light he really nails
the mystic stuff, and My Sweet Lord was a big surprise smash
but he got done for nicking the riff.

I said George's greatest moment was on Revolver
and that really seemed to pluck her strings.
When I Need You came on I asked her to dance
so we swayed a bit over by the potted plants.

I've heard women say he's wet or sad, but on Taxman he gets
so riled and hunky, and other places he gives you
raunchy licks and wild boogying kicks, and if he wasn't
twice the player Lennon was then I'm a pickled cucumber.

I said: 'I've got this book of cuttings back at my place.'
'Oh, have you?' she says.
'Stacks,' I says. 'From all over, some in Japanese.
Would you like to come round and see them?'
'No,' she says. 'I'm going home to practise my Fish Posture.'

*Glyn Wright*

## STRAWBERRY FIELDS, DEAD MAN'S VALLEY

They come down our road from Penny Lane
press cheeks to bars at Dovedale school
then want to know the way to Strawberry Fields,
and you have to say, slowly, talking foreign,
that it's really quite hard to explain:
it's not an easy place to get to.

In the song it says forever, but big blond Billy
is hairless now, and Fred will wince at ulcers,
and Kite was last heard of in another country.
No one seems to know what became of Wendy
or her sisters, and all the rest who romped
the grass, monkied in the bushes and the trees.

Dead Man's Valley, the sledge hill and the Towers;
Strawberry Fields and Priory woods, out of bounds
places you giggled in. Jumping walls and fences.
Larking down a lane where phantom pipers blew
on misty nights, swinging skywards from fat
silver branches until the old rope snapped.

Billy, it was, who crashed to earth, but Fred
climbed on stage wailing Twist and Shout
and we all nicked brown ale from the offy, messed
with girls on the golf course after dark. Skinny Linda
in the bushes with a lad whose old man played the cello,
us lying out on grass, Kite saying all the stars were dead.

When long-haired Julia rolled up in a Butlin's
laundry van, waving one of Lennon's big harps
I sucked it at the mirror going: You know I
love you, so if there's anything that you want.
Years on, a piece for orchestra in his memory,
slammed piano lid played the fatal shots.

You tell them there isn't much to see: they built
on Strawberry Fields, the iron gates are padlocked.
In the song it says forever, but over there
is dream now, different realm. And other voices call:

Imagine. Eleanor Rigby. Jude and Sadie. Yesterday.
All the people and the things that went before.
Remember. Maggie Mae. They have taken her away
and she'll never walk down Lime Street any more.

*Glyn Wright*

## TRAVELLING THROUGH PEPPERLAND

You just put on this bright uniform and joined the band,
all the orchestra were there with the lonely and the famous.
I passed Oscar Wilde and Huxley, Edgar Allan Poe.
Someone said that lawyers had stopped Elvis coming
but Mae West turned up with Tarzan, and Lenny Bruce
took time off from his tired drug-bust routines.

The horn player had an early blow but overdid it
then the drummer wants to know what would happen
if he couldn't sing in tune, and the proper singer,
looking distant, sees a sungirl in a diamond sky
but she's carried off too soon on fading bass strings.

Spicy congas for the Cornman; crafty twister spins away
to make space for the Weeper sighing for all broken-
hearted parents: the strugglers and the self-deniers who
had to watch their wilful darlings dancing to a crazy rhythm.

I saw weird circus folk and a drifting tabla player,
heard the clarinets of contentment hum for ageing lovers,
but that fiendish cock of dawn burst in with a snigger
as the meter maid's piano rolled off down some sideroad.

Morning was a frightening place, throwing at you memory
and cymbals, confessions and shrieks, nagging horns
and suffering guitars that moaned for the laughing singer
who's read the news, the nightmare man who jumps ruffled
meek and gasping at his alarm clock's shrill command.

Jamming fiddles finished tangled with the woodwind
as horns roared on until the last pianos crashed
and the buses of a thousand future rush hours
carried us away in all directions
        of boom
        and silence.

*Glyn Wright*

## THE SIGN IN CELTIC LETTERING

It was leaning against a wall
At the rear of the factory
Where the cars used to park,
The sign in celtic lettering.
It had been there for some time
And it was starting to warp,
Its cream paint had lost its shine,
The lettering still stood out though,
Dark blue against the cream,
The tops of the letters all sliced
Stylishly off to give the effect,
But rain and sun had seen to it.
It had lost its initial freshness.
Hopeless really.
But it had been painted with care,
Someone had made an effort,
There was no doubt.

Behind the wall it leant against
There was a non-descript garden
With a few sickly flowers and shrubs,
A strip of earth and a tussocky lawn
Which lead to the rear of a house.
There were pegs on a line and the grass
Was still wet after a heavy shower,
The clothes-line was beaded with droplets;
I tried to get through the wall of the house
Wondering what the lounge was like
And whether there was a sagging clothes-line
Beaded with droplets in there too,
And a few pegs, a red one, a yellow and a blue
And maybe tussocky clumps of grass
Growing up through a worn carpet,
Shrubs, a few sickly flowers;
And maybe in the hall a kind of leather sofa
Piled high with a variety of memorabilia,
An heraldic hawk's head stick perhaps,
Gleaming japanned boxes, a peacock's feather,
Old and ornate stopped clocks,

With sepia-coloured photographs in frames,
A gas mask, a bayonet, a box camera,
A bakelite radio, and one long-playing record,
Sergeant Pepper's Lonely Hearts Club Band,
a thin slice, its illustrated cover
and that 4/4 rhythm locked in there,
Nowhere to go:
Next to all this, leaning against a chair
Piled high with magazines and newspapers
There's a warped cream coloured sign
In celtic lettering.

*David Iveson*

## PEPPER COVER

Peter Blake and Jann Haworth baked
a pizza peppered with famous faces,
assorted heroes and villains,
some faked, some wax,
some black and white
when the money ran out.

No, listen to this.
It's stereophonic.
You can hear the guitar
moving across the room.

We sat on the floor and marvelled,
tracing George's path around the sofa,
his skilful negotiation of the lamp stand,
pondered backward messages at the inside rim.

It won't be any good
if it's based on that meditation stuff,
my brother had pronounced,
being a brother and knowing all things.

We picked up a piece of Peter's peppered pizza
and went into a dream.

*Michael Cunningham*

# A DAY IN THE HOSPITAL

The fog that morning held
like sleep,
my father looked old,
one eye watery, the other patched.

My mother banged her head
as we got into the car:
'How did you do that?' I asked.
'How did I do that?' she said
as I turned the radio on.

And though the news
was rather sad,
I just had to laugh
driving through the smalltalk.

Hospital windows blinked
in the bandaged light.
I thought of you last night.

A crowd of people stood and stared

as I caught them both
mirrored:
he, looking ahead,
upright as a blindman;
she gently guiding,
eyes fixed on his face.

Nobody was really sure if...

the image held
like morning fog,
like sleep
sweet sleep.
      Somebody spoke

*Paul Butler*

# IF YOU WERE THERE

or if you can imagine
being there in 1967
when all you need is love
possessed the airwaves
heartwaves   if you were there
when they threw a party
in the television studio
invited all the world along
and if you chanted
crosslegged on the floor
with love's new symbol
blooming from your hand
or the long silks of your hair
and if flowing in your clothes
you knew the light
loose airiness of freedom
if someone passed around
a bottle or a joint
which multiplied
like the five loaves and fishes
and if it seemed a peace factory
was in production there
and everywhere
if you saw hope ballooning
and the old dry thoughts
of parents and politicians
shredded by
the Lennon and McCartney word
and tumbling lightly
from the misty incensed air
till they were old dead leaves
you crushed beneath your feet
if you were there
or if you can imagine
being there in 1967
join the circle

*Chris Banks*

## VARIATION ON A
## LENNON AND McCARTNEY SONG

Love, love, love,
Love, love, love,
Love, love, love,
Dooby doo dooby doo,
All you need is love,
Dooby dooby doo,
All you need is love,
Dooby dooby doo,
All you need is love, love
Or, failing that, alcohol.

*Wendy Cope*

## HELLO GOODBYE

Tea-with-the-Queen smiles
had not brought the permissive society
to our house.

Remember 'Hello, Goodbye'?
We played it over and over
on the *auto* setting of Dad's record-player
45 r.p.m.
thinking he was out,
until we knew all the words
right down to the 'Wah-wah'wah-wah
do you say...'

Then we flipped it over,
got hit by
'I am the Walrus',
and you went rushing to Mum
yelling, 'It says on the record
'bout a naughty girl pulls her knickers down!'

And in he came.

Didn't even listen to it.
Didn't even give it a chance.
Hello. Goodbye.

GIVE IT TO ME.
NO.

'You say yes, I say no.
You say why, and I say...'

Remember the scratch
as he snatched it off the turntable?
And that rubber-mat-thing
went skeetering off the side?

'Oh. Oh no.'

Remember you ran after him,
watched the black disc buckle on the fire,
pop its flames roaring into the chimney,
Beatles bubbling to nothing
on hot coals?

Back at his record-player,
one of his 78's: we staggered around the table
with our arms out wide:

'He's got the whole wide world in His hands.'

*Russell Milner*

## THE CAT ON THE HILL

sees the violets beneath
and the eyes in her head
see foxgloves turn red.

Nobody wants to know her
they can see she's just a cat
and they never hear her mewing
but the cat on the hill

sees the violets beneath
and the eyes in her head
see foxgloves turn red.

*Tom Browning*

## CONVERSATION ON A TRAIN

I'm Shirley, she's Mary.
We're from Swansea
(if there was a horse there
it'd be a one-horse town
but there isn't even that).
We're going to Blackpool
Just the week. A bit late I know
But then there's the Illuminations
Isn't there? No, never been before.
Paris last year. Didn't like it.
Too expensive and nothing there really.

Dirty old train isn't it?
And not even a running buffet.
Packet of crisps would do
Change at Crewe
Probably have to wait hours
For the connection, and these cases
Are bloody heavy.
And those porters only want tipping.
Reminds you of Paris that does
Tip tip tip all the time.
Think you're made of money over there.

Toy factory, and Mary works in a shop.
Grocers. Oh it's not bad
Mind you the money's terrible.
Where are you from now?
Oh aye, diya know the Beatles then?
Liar!
And what do you do for a living?
You don't say.
Diya hear that Mary?
Well I hope you don't go home
And write a bloody poem about us.

*Roger McGough*

## CAN'T EVEN BUY IT IN GLASGOW

I thought it would be cool
to write a poem about the Beatles,
so I curled up in bed in the foetal
position and prepared some lines in my head.
But the connections must have got confused,
for I thought about you instead.

The beat of your drum was insistent;
made me go weak at the knees,
but your eyes weren't 'groupie' resistant,
you turned out to be a great tease.
So when John stayed in bed with Yoko
and Paul escaped from the nest,
I pushed you from a tenement window;
my mates were dead impressed.

Now I'm here in my cell
singing love songs;
there's one with a hollow refrain,
if love was all that was needed,
I'd be out in the world again.

*Genista Lewes*

# BEATLES

*The Listener*, 3 October 1968

William Huskisson, President of the Board of Trade, was standing between the lines in Liverpool welcoming the first train. 'I declare this railway well and truly – AARAGH!' SPLAT! It was the best death scene since an eagle dropped a tortoise on the head of Aeschylus (THUNK!) but it only rates 21 words in Hunter Davies' *The Beatles*, although however already this official biography is a long trudge compared with Michael Braun's sprinting Penguin (*Love Me Do*), yet notwithstanding perhaps there's some fair scenery along the way, especially when Mr Davies shows how various songs were fitted together. So much for criticism.

The average Englishman wakes up one morn-
ing to find himself born,
and starting to explore
what his body is for
finds there's rhythm and blues
in his shoes
and that's news
because a few years ago
the average British toe
could only go
slow slow quick slow slow.
Now the offbeat of the heartbeat
is the children's choice
and the human voice
can shake while it sings and twist and shout
because some of the fear's flown out.

Most of us are mostly afraid –
Murder Incorporated has to be paid
and there's terror in the bone
because of Al Capone
from Canterbury, Baby-Face Calvin
and the spiritual Chicago of Rome.
And though you chain up the door
of your rentokilled home –
Matthew Mark Luke and John

surround the bed that you lie on with dread,
each of them armed with a nuclear warhead.

But the Beatles roared along
at the wheel of an independently suspended song
and they saw the rows of English feet
and they knew that feet without a beat are just meat,
so they rolled down the windows to let the word be heard
and every time they passed a naked human has-been
they all shouted out – it's a clean machine.
Jehovah, Jesus, Holy Ghost and Ringo Starr,
Four-faced jubilee weeping in the public bar,
Suddenly flowering home-made submarine –
Shift all the slag heaps from Aberfan to Esher Green.
I'm not trying to paint you a quartet of saints
or musical Guevaras.
But the standard of loving has
plopped through the bottom of the graph.
So the few who do any kind of thing
that shakes out the horrors
are quadruply welcome
especially if they make us laugh.

The fashion-go-round of the underground
may forsake them,
the Army or the CIA may take them,
but we'll meet again...

So to the point as fast as possible. When Allen Ginsberg was last over here, he gave a reading of Blake and Ginsberg at the Roundhouse, Chalk Farm, at a time when all honest chalk farmers were in bed dreaming of the sprouting pink, blue and white lengths of chalk which decorate the dusty fields around the blackboard forest. Between poems Ginsberg talked about fear. he said that 10 or 15 years ago he had been full of fear, but that he'd worked at cutting down his terror ration and had changed until he was hardly afraid of anything. I sat in the audience and felt the lump of fear which I always carry diminish.

The Beatles appear to be moving, zigzag, in the Ginsberg direction. They've already shown some courage in a traditionally cowardly trade – for in pop music the aim is to be loved by everyone, villains included. Maybe it was foolhardiness when they filmed their own *Magical Mystery*

*Tour.* It contained some images – policemen holding hands on a top of a concrete bunker or shelter while The Beatles played below in Disney masks – which were way beyond the heads of most of the critics. The progress of their songs from 'Please please me' (instantly likeable and who, at the time, could ask for anything more) to 'Penny Lane' (poetry) and 'A day in the life' and 'I am the walrus' (adventurous poetry) has been an exciting voyage to follow. After all, everyone knew Francis Chichester wasn't going to fall off the edge of the world, but The Beatles might.

Snipers from the press will keep trying to shoot them down and keep missing, because The Beatles have more to offer than the press. Most people, without envy, wish them good luck on their journey. More than that, many people hope that their courage increases, and not just for the sake of their art. There are obviously more important issues.

Take one of these. For many years England has been unofficially, sometimes shamefacedly and often silently racialist. Then along came Enoch Powell, strumming on the nerves of the nation, speaking the language of cold sweat. Suddenly he became the first popular politician since the war – has anyone else so rallied the Right? Enoch Powell has changed and will continue to change English politics from blatantly selfish to patently lunatic. The weakness of both Heath's and Wilson's responses proves how scared they are.

I'm not suggesting that Powellism could be stopped if The Beatles applied their considerable wits to a record called *Enoch.* But they would be heard. They would also lose votes. They would be subject to a great deal of hatred. They have taken risks in the past, but this would be a higher risk, one that might mean imprisonment (in a bad future) or might, by amplifying the small chorus of brave voices, mean that the future might be less bad.

*Adrian Mitchell*

## LEFT OUT

All I remember from 1968
Is peanut butter, Thunderbirds and a badly painted Beatles plate.
My mother talked a lot, my father let her.
But she never mentioned student riots,
Or a desire to change society for the better.

*Tim Bradford*

## WHAT'S THE NEW MARY JANE?

*She looks as an African queen,*
*she eating twelve chapatis and cream,*
*she tastes as Mongolian lamb,*
*she coming from Aldebaran*

The day you went mad, I came back across the sea
to find you laughing, and talking to God,
unreal as a sixties TV play,
a script as if written by David Mercer,
except that it was all so horribly exact.

Daylight, not studio lights, lit your
star-struck face, eyes focused on the infinite,
blank as the sky, and then those endless weeks,
plunging into nightmare.

No use for food – remember the five hours we waited
for potatoes, your reckless assurances, the way
you caressed that knife – so sustenance on alcohol,

and that bootleg tape you played over and over,
like Syd Barrett fixated on a riff,
John Lennon's own prefiguration,

*'I'm dead already, you know the reason why'.*

over and over that acid distortion,
clunky piano, Frank's wild accordian,
psychedelic Swanee whistle, wackily bored vocals,

*She catch Patagonian pancakes*
*with that one and gin party makes.*

Nonsense mad nonsensical, breaking down into
mechanical laughter, as if from a block of painted wood,
chords that fail to resolve,
screams that harmonise.
A dish you fed on until the ambulance came,
like holy writ, your childhood deities

grown old and strange, like us all.

*To fly all day and sing in tune and not hear what I heard.*
*To see you all around me and to take you by the hand*
*and lead you to a brand new world that lately has been banned,*
*to build things never built before, and do things never done,*
*and just before it's over it's really just begun*

Reports of your mind reforming have so far proved
misguided.

*Brian Hinton*

## TWO POEMS CALLED WAREHOUSE

1.
The days when I knocked on doors and ran off
have long since gone, as have the times I queued

to watch films like *The Guns of Navarone*
and *The Dambusters*. Somewhere in there

my dad warned me not to listen to The Beatles:
did I want to end up on drugs? Later,

at the warehouse, I came to be known as
*a good worker*. I never expected

more than seemed likely: a bunch of mates like
Paul and John, maybe, a few bouncing bombs.


2.
My dad would be shaving by five; I'd shaved
the night before. I'd make us both coffee

and sit in my overall, hands round mug.
We drove to work in silence, more or less;

he was hard of hearing from the steelworks
he'd been made redundant from years before.

In the army he'd driven officers
from point A to point B, still had the air

of that driver. When we reached the warehouse,
he'd go to his place and I'd go to mine.

*Geoff Hattersley*

# THE WHITE POEM

*Rupert M. Loydell*

# THE NAMES OF THE BEATLES


GEORGE JOHN PAUL RICHARD


(wears rings)
**hence:**


```
                    RINGOGOGO
                 RINGO my  RINGO
              HONJ  love         JNOH
            ULAP        choirboy      PALU
          GROGEE          sad brown      EEGORG
        GNLR              maureen starkey      RLNG
      JUG         the fool with the sad brown eyes    GUJ
     P                who cares if he can drum          P
   NOU                    yoko ono                     OUN
   IH                    patti harrison                 HI
  O                 choirboy with a heart of brass       O
  PE        pray for us sinners now and in the hour of   EP
  R                     minim triplets                   R
   OU                    linda mccartney                UO
    UO        don't come around leave me alone         OU
      H                voice like washed gravel       H
        AE                cynthia lennon           EA
          LG             your bird can sing      GL
```

PGJRAEOIUOHNLRNGGOE

this is the mandala


64

stuart sutcliffe pete best george martin brian epstein
**OM**
these are the names of the lost
**OM**
Somewhere in the sound
**OM**
at the speed of sound
**OM**
o what is that sound
**OM**
the sound of the river
**OM**
the mersey sound
**OM**
lost in the traffic
**OM**
lost in the volume
**OM**
lost in the screaming at shay
**OM**
the names
marcliffe ange sutep bristuest steinbart  tegeorpetin
the lost
the mantra


**have you heard:**
the news from hamburg
the new sound
echoes from the cavern
the news today oh boy
george and the maharishi
they're all on dope
no they're fucking not
with diamonds
paul's symbolically dead
they've split up
they're getting it together
they've split up
john's been blown away
they're getting it together
they've split they've split they've split
ringo's making movies

**all right george:**

```
                 GORIN oh  NIROG
             HONJ   money        JNOH
         ULAP          can'tbuy      PALU
       GROGEE           sun shine    EEGORG
     GNLR           cynthia lennon        RLNG
   JUG                maureen starkey      GUJ
  P                    patti harrison              P
 NOU                    yoko ono                 OUN
 IH                  linda mccartney              HI
O            the choirboy with heart of brass        O
 PE         pray for us sinners now and in the hour of    EP
 R                fool with the sad brown eyes        R
  OU                    the prophet              UO
    UO        the eggman the walrus            OU
      H        don't come around leave me alone    H
       AE        voice like washed gravel    EA
         LG          your bird can sing    GL
```

PGJRAEOIUOHNLRNGGOE

this is the mandala

**mantra:**

**OM**

if they'd been a brummie band we could have loved them
bus tickets smudging in the rain
we can
work it
out

the last enigma

*Tony Charles*

## LOVING RINGO

If you thought you were clever
you might pine for John –
a night with never-never
eyes and nothing on.

For the wine-and-roses kind,
romance à la France,
it was George who'd meet your mind
and request a dance.

And Paul was for – all the rest.
He had the nice smile,
the kindly eyes and the best
tunes – but not my style.

So in my fourteenth summer,
disdaining the horde,
it had to be the drummer
I madly adored.

Ringo was the one for those
wanting to be wives,
his tonsils, jewels and nose
ours for all our lives.

he faithfully kept the beat,
he funnily spoke,
for his was the driving seat
and the fabbest joke.

So I heard when I met Jim
my heart go Bingo!
'cause Jim was the spit of him,
...we learned love's lingo

acting naturally,
till onto my left third finger –oh,
way back in August '70 –
I felt his ring go.

*Elizabeth Moore*

## STILL AROUND

I find it difficult remembering
faces, names, appointments, when to water
potted plants. And various other things
but what they are I can't remember either.

But can remember tunes, who wrote them – Brahms,
Giles Farnaby. What trees look like in snow.
A floating fear. Your smile. Composers' names.
A party – village hall – my mother made me go –

the Beatles blaring. Rave, but not my scene.
Far too far out to dance, I sank and drowned,
passed over by a yellow submarine.
You smile – which means we must be still around,

you and me, the Beatles too. You smiling.
Their songs (now on CD). And me still drowning.

*James Turner*

## BLUE STRATOS

One sniff can send me swimming down that fuzzy tube,
swallowing years in seconds,
catching people like stars.
Feeling my way along rooftops,
delving into pockets of yesterday's gold.

The complete chronicles of Narnia,
tie-on roller skates, Ker-Plunk!,
sticky tarmac on brown sandals,
plastered kneed and unbrushed hair.

Home of the record player,
big sister's room. Real bras, Miss Selfridge,
pink lipgloss.
78, 45, 33, it puts its arm around them all,
dad's old records; Needles and Pins, Carpenters,
The Beatles.

My first men.
An audio love affair, no strings.
I kissed their flat faces,
chased them round that vinyl circle,
missed them when the needle slid back.

We moved, grew big. Stack stereos, then CDs.
Married three dimensional men,
keep records tucked away in the attic.
I go up there, now and again,
sniff Blue Stratos. Swim.

*Gemma Green*

# BEATLEMANIA

She hasn't made a telephone call
Since nineteen sixty four
Now quiet as a browsing library mouse
She mimes to old song lyrics from adolescence
Drops pennies into brand new
And battered subway guitar cases
Younger than grey hair the last scream
Fainted on her lips somewhere
In the middle of Beatlemania

You were never one of my heroes Pau
I was into cowboys, and cowboys
Didn't play bass guitars
I wasn't jealous, even when my girlfriend
Looked over my shoulder at photographs
Of you on the bedroom wall
Though I hated it everytime she screamed
Especially when the police came
And introduced me to their interrogations,
handcuffs, and saliva snarling dogs
Who were definitely not vegetarian

The first time my girlfriend's decibels
Redecorated the neighborhood
I thought a demon had opened
The lid of the Dansette
Laryngitis was number one in the
National Health Service charts that year
The year she kissed you
On the lips of a record cover
Cowboys sang songs about
Cowgirls from Colorado

And the girl next door to everyone
Fell in love with fame,
Rock and roll, and your shadow
Was Krakatoa in the time of McCartney
And the multi-promiscuous voice
Reverberated from millions of teenage mouths

Tuneless acapella tongue hearts
That relegated Casanova and Romeo
To a duet of B sides

*Kenny Knight*

## THE BEATLE GENERATION

I'm baffled about the Beatles
– I'm beating about the bush
Oh Ringo Starr – do I know who you are?
    And the other bright lads – have they faded?
– I can't even remember what they did –

    I'm scratching around in my memory
        And I've found
        On the ground
        At the bottom
    The fantastic – but accurate truth!

    The stars of the faraway sixties
        Are scintillating still!
    On tape and on disc they frolic and frisk
        So the Beatles can charm us at will.

But we poor poets who are only on paper
    – We will go yellow with age
And if anyone fetches us down from the shelf
    And turns us over page after page
Back with a bump we will probably go
    And there we will probably stay
But John, Paul, George and Ringo
    Can still turn yesterday into today.

*Elma Mitchell*

## ROBIN SAID THAT JOHN LENNON'S
## HALF BROTHER'S LOOK-ALIKE
## WAS REALLY FUNNY AT SCHOOL

When the teacher was out of the room
John Lennon's half brother's look-alike
would stand up in front of everyone
and say the word *deaf* out loud.
He was a dead-ringer for a not-too-close relative
of a very famous person, but even so,
the word deaf was a not-OK word.
But this twin sort of person pretended it was
the kind of word that let you feel OK
and not embarrassed, like *sky* or *wood* or *yellow*.
Sometimes he tried other not-OK words
like *crippled*, *dumb* and *blind*
but he was afraid to use any volume
with these words in case someone, a teacher, for instance,
or someone who looked like a teacher,
passing in the corridor, would be able to hear.
He mouthed these words in such a clever way
that lip readers might have thought
he was actually saying some OK-words
like *diamonds*, *Norwegian*, and *submarine*.

The teacher, who everyone knew was deaf,
stood watching from the doorway
and managed to laugh a bit at some of the jokes
and seemed to pick up a few of the OK-words.
But the word *deaf* was hardly in earshot,
and the other not-OK words
got lost in slots between words
which were, well, just fairly-OK.

Then the teacher came into the room and said
'I wouldn't record it, if I were you.
Not everyone's deaf or dumb or thick.
Blind people can hear, you know.
And the tune, if it's really a tune, is crap.'

He said the words *blind* and *deaf* and *crap*
as if they were all OK-words,
just straight, unsentimental sorts of words,
and John Lennon's half brother's look-alike
repeated the words just by mouthing them.
Blind, deaf, crap. Blind, deaf, crap.
he said them with feeling and drama
but he never gave them a tune,
yet they looked like a song if you watched him
shaping the words over and over,
belting them out like an opera singer you'd see on TV,
maybe on twenty screens all at once,
in a TV shop with the sound turned off.

Then he added a drum machine, an echo box,
flashing lights with coloured gels.
He put in bits of synthesised, not-quite-OK sounds,
and a few, definitely-OK low pitched vibrations.
He didn't skimp on throbs, beats or special effects.
He had the words *dazzle* and *razzle* on his mind
and *bazazz* and *shanannagans*,
but they never got into his song.

The song was a humdinger,
sure to make the charts, he thought.
But would the meaning come over, he wondered?
Would they get it if they couldn't hear the words?
Would it catch on without a tune?
Would it be played in lifts and at shopping malls,
with only words, if it didn't have a melody?
What if the words were only mimed
and no one could see the mouth of the mime?
Would the words be OK, or would the words be not-OK?

John Lennon's half brother's dead-ringer
was very funny at school right up to this moment
and then he stopped.

*Linda Chase*

## CLASS ACT

'bumped into history today,
a million punters down the Cavern Club,
          you couldn't get them all inside,
                  there'd be no place to hide,
seems that almost all the so-called regulars
                      had lied,

so much for turning on...'

the line's gone dead –
a flickering black-and-white
of screaming girls and good old Harold
and George bemusedly young –
nothing so unusual as the recently past

but was a time they still had lines
and Hank's was crossed on the Fab Four
– OK, more proletarian than Cliff,
NOT AMERICAN like white trash Elvis,
into Peace, and jokes at the Royals' expense,
you could almost give them five for that
but what about the MBEs?
the Maharishi, Yoko Ono,
the fucking vegetarianism?
the sixties made it hard to grade our heroes
and the line broke around the Beatles;
with them the classless society went nuclear,
the Beatles were a commisar's hell,
and Hank's testimony stands mute of malice

– what do you *really* think about them, Tam?

– I remember that *Sergeant Pepper*
   fucking art college crap;
   I preferred the Rolling Stones,
   you knew where you were with them boys –
   pissing up against a wall

*Gordon Wardman*

75

## FORBIDDEN FRUITS

sometime round about Brezhnev's sixth Order of Lenin
Hank was in Moscow on business,
where, as a special treat
(after the compulsory collective farm
and the equally compulsory Bolshoi),
he got taken to a Party-only night club

*Dean Tempest, International Vocalist,*
*Greatest English Act since the Beatles*

Dean was a redundant miner from Barnsley
with an unusually imaginative agent
who did a fair Tom Jones impersonation
to accordion and balalaika accompaniment

Dean reckoned Russia was a right good laugh

– just tell them everything's by the Beatles,
   pal, you can't go wrong

– what happens if they check?

– you ever tried buying a Beatles record here?

under socialism, comrade, we have
full employment,
         no crises of overproduction

*Gordon Wardman*

## YOU DO REMEMBER THE BEATLES?

Yes, you could buy their breath in cans
inhale endless possibilities,
such a hunger –
Penny Lane – brilliant morning
eyes pierced by diamonds
ticket to ride
teendom forever
on the top of the bus.

I couldn't keep up
got dropped off
at the pick your own hostel
missed out on the trips
to the nowhere wood
of foolish, serious obsessions,
the hard days midsummer night's
dream of instant zen.

Was it Mr Wilson jangled their medals
in his raincoat pocket while
a nursery rhyme submarine circled the stars
the whole human hearts' club shut inside?
All those white faces.
Then the glasses on the sidewalk
clear as yesterday
fixed them firmly in history

make 'em laugh, make 'em cry
they couldn't fail.
Only this morning I heard
the still small voice
of old Miss Rigby, 94,
demolishing the Kareoke
at Age Concern, LOVE ME DO
she sang, LOVE ME DO...

*Wendy McBride*

## YES SON, BUT ELEANOR RIGBY COULD SING

My Dad thinks Magritte's paintings are the work
of a weirdo

but I think back to those astonishing
days of Beatlemania

when the goldfish were given a year off
at the Cherry Wake – every prize was a Beatles mug –

when the Media bombarded us with
something that was actually worthy

when prolific popular culture met Art head on
for close on ten colossal years

and I remember my Dad marvelling at the line
'kept her face in a jar by the door'

'It's only like Eleanor Rigby Dad' I defend
Magritte's surrealism in the powerful court of
Messrs Lennon and McCartney.

'Yes son, but Eleanor Rigby could sing.'

*Gary Boswell*

# EPITAPH FOR A 'SIXTIES GROUPIE

Ringo, Paul, George and John
bless the bed that I lie on –
this stage door here's a lonely place
to wait for the Beloved Face.

Although it's been a hard night's day,
I still believe in yesterday
and know that somewhere up above
it's true that all you need is love.

So take me by celestial cab
to the place where everything is fab
and, hung with diamonds, set me high,
to shine, like Lucy, in the sky.

*Anthony Watts*

## HEADBAND 1

TV interference. I can't napalm the whole
of Stoke-on-Trent! Better make some coffee
and sit at the typewriter. You know,
I wrote one about Vincent Price.
Had him shopping for Christmas gifts,
in Wyoming. Then a dog charged him,
made him fall. He went down,
shouting expletives. Not true,
of course. But who cares? Well, old seal-clubber,
old tusk collector, is there anything
in the slightly charred warehouse of my mind?
Try this. The Windmill is a
clod's throw from here; and probably a train ride
and a hike through wilderness,
from wherever you are? The landlord looks like
John Doe with migraine. He's
from Stafford (what can you do?)
and likes to talk about ballroom dancing
as perfected by him and Joan. Well, last night,
or was it last Summer? I
was sitting in the beer garden,
with a pint of moderate. My
expected date had come to seem
like someone who'd fell from a cliff,
in a black and white film. I went
back to the bar. Vodka helped me to forget
and then to remember... That bus-stop has probably been bought
by a Japanese businessman. But in those days,
it was by the Midland Bank. I arrived,
yellow suitcase; in shades and a denim suit. Wheels came.
Got on. Saw Jim. 'Are you going to Wolverhampton?'
he said. 'There's four thousand going down.' I told him
I was bound for Torquay: meeting the gang
by the Palm Court Hotel. He showed me a knife
he'd got in his jacket. 'There'll be trouble,'
he said. He didn't know that *he was* the trouble:
the north south east and west of it... Torquay:
had time to burn. Sat in a deckchair on the prom.
Two hundred lads in blue and white scarves

ran by: most of them throwing chairs into the sea.
They were a mob in need of a mob in need of them...
Helen King was sitting on the hotel steps. She wore a caliper
and, man, she was beautiful. A mate with her: striped dress,
headband; couldn't stop saying 'Far out'... 'Where are they?'
I said. Helen, laughing, said: 'Fred's in jail. The others
are swimming'. Well, old misanthrope, better push this along.
Let's say the afternoon was a drifting boat: I was in it,
Helen was in it, headband was in it. Let's say
the night was a hovercraft and it dumped us on the beach:
drunk, drinking, clapping, singing 'Hey Jude'.

*Peter Lane*

## ON THE ROOF OF THE WORLD

'Hey Jude' was the longest single, up to that time,
ever released. It sweats off, chorus like a mantra.
The times are changing. New musics divide the audience
and skirts are longer, but it's a bright London shopping day
when the traffic stops. Only a black cab moves
gingerly through the crowd, like a toy cruiser nudging weed,
and we're all craning upwards: planks and scaffolding
on the townhouse roof and the clipped, drifting music
the Beatles play. It is their last concert,
though nobody knows this. George twangs his Fender, John
hammers-off on his Epiphone, Paul stomps
with his violin-bodied fretless bass and Ringo, dreamed up
by a manager who died a long time ago, kicks the years
out of his bass drum padded with a rug. How sweet

it would have been, someone will write, to watch them
play the Marquee, this funky little rock'n'roll band.
They are so far above us, we can hardly see them.
They are playing for God. They are playing for cameras
because the show's outgrown the road. We can't believe it.
Tomorrow's papers will acclaim a British institution.
I'll read them and imagine I was there like everyone.
They are already going out of fashion. There's nothing left
but acrimony, separation, lawsuits. The last great single,
'The Ballad of John and Yoko', will be John and Paul
alone, hurrying in midsummer heat, the way it was at the start.
Nobody knows this. They have climbed too far to get back
anywhere we might be among the crowd who clap then drift apart
when the helmeted bobbies have the amps turned off.

*Lachlan Mackinnon*

# HOW GOOD THINGS WERE

'When we get in a studio, even on the worst day,
I'm still playing bass, Ringo's still drumming
and we're still there you know.'
                    – Paul McCartney, Autumn 1969

Maybe we forgot how good things were
Forgot how good the Beatles were
Forgot how good school was in its reluctant way
Forgot how good it was walking home
from the dancehall in the rain, last bus gone
How funny it was, your mother screaming
Look at your blouse! It's undone!
Forgot the parties, the hangovers, screaming in bed
on Sunday afternoons
But worse, we forgot how good we were, how brilliantly
we shone, until too late, beyond our will to save
Our mortgaged hearts had lost the beat, were set like stone

*Patric Cunnane*

# WITH THE BEATLES

Long Sundays. Corona high. Picnic bars and Pick of the Pops.
A sofa stage for three of us – nine, ten, all wanting to be Paul. Then.
My sister press ganged as Ringo.
Sound.
Mersey sound.
Sound as a pound. Hohner bass badges.
My parents bought the singles, sent back Twist and Shout.

And later, Magical Mystery Tour was too much.
Too much for me, the Obla-Di's, The Yellow Submarine,
The Octopus's Garden In The Sea.
Sixteen, seventeen – Sundays shorter.
It quietly slipped away.

Nice, English pop pitched The Young Ones against The Boys,
Until you sucked in soul. All the fizz and bite of sherbet lemons
Got three generations dancing, still,
And a Giaconda smile on the acceptable face of rock and roll.

Karaoke nights, everyone knows the words
And where they were when they heard Lennon died.
No revolution, an institution.
Sound. Dead sound.
Let it be, so, let it be.

*Jeremy Rogers*

## LET IT BE

Moptop boys
hold hands with me
and dance…

Moptop boys
dance with me
and sing…

Here are some drugs.
Here are some women.
Here is a guru.
Here is fame
and money
and sex
and noise
and screams
filling the air.

Here is the life
you can't handle.

Moptop boys
grow your hair
and sleep with me…

Moptop boys
take LSD
and trip with me…

Moptop boys
chant for peace
make art for me…

Here is the past.
Here is the future.
Here is the next album.
And here is the film
of the end:

the rooftop jam sessions,
the pathetic arguments,
the band in disarray;
the realisation that
the music has gone and
there is nothing to say.

Here is where
friendships fail.
Here are four
*ex*-Beatles.

Here is the life
you can't handle,
the music
that won't go away.

*Rupert M. Loydell*

## SNAPSHOTS

*for John Lennon*

swigs of whiskey
along a snow-packed road
slipping   giggling   tipsy
at the party rubber soul
under the skin
against the bone
the scrape of your voice
chafing raw nerves

ma belle
he sang as we danced
and i wished
i was called michelle
instead of chrissy


.


paul was pinned to my wall
paul i screamed for
his smile slipping inside
warm and snaky   eyes
into which a young girl's body
could slide could longingly fall
drown even   what did it matter

today
     i see
the unremarkable face
     of a hamster

but   you   john   you


.


at the church eisteddfodd in 1964
andrea wore orange angora
read two of your poems

instead of the usual walter de la mare
caused a stir among the crimplene
and brylcreemed hair

you should have been there
in fact
        you should have been
                the vicar


        .


snapped before you disappear

you're frozen here among a blur
of followers   icon in an afghan
who walks towards the camera
one arm held out as if to bless

a long shadow traces your steps
your eyes are full of what you wish
you didn't know

                        i want to stop you
walking out of the picture
to a future
        when you are not here

        *Chris Banks*

## JOHN LENNON

Arriving out of nowhere. Retrospect
reads revolution into accident,
somebody breaking into a decade
to invent the sixties, stand on its head

post-war inertia. The black knitted tie,
fringe to the eyebrows, stack heeled boots replaced
by kaftans, Indian beads, an acid trip
standing a forest in the sky;
a little girl rides on an elephant
out of her dream into another dream.
The universe fits neatly in his eye.

Banging a piano in an empty room,
New York outside, it all happened too fast.
He searches for a melody
to clarify the changes. he's withdrawn
into another vision, white on white
or black on black, both are the same
keys to invisibility.
The songs are messages and they return
to us who listen as the sunlight falls
over the late part of a century
deciding what is gone and what will last.

*Jeremy Reed*

# NEW YEAR'S EVE '93

Well here it is
the last one of the year

Ready Steady Go and
Malibu

Brian Jones' grin
P.J. Proby's grin

Where is it?

Screams bring nothing
back

Screams don't stop it

That's why / it's so
good

Don't knock me over
tonight

Though I might be a
bit slow in crossing

Though tonight everything
might be a bit black and
white

It's all payed for many
times over

Film of fire / is not
exactly cold
John

*Tim Allen*

**THE ONLY RECORD
OF THE BEATLES I HAVE
IS THE BEATLES SEASONS
PLAYED BAROQUE**

Early 60s
and from the back of my Bantam
(me, square tie on square bike)
Carl shouts, 'They're good,
they're going to be great,
Great with a capital G.'

They'll not go far,' I scream
and think
Bach's Great
and Beethoven
da da da dum
and the Good Life
with Geese and a Goat
and my Grandfather a Jones
and the Great View
from the Lleyn.

From the pillion,
'yeah, yeah, yeah.'
'They'll never make it,' I shout.

That evening we look
at the Wicklow Mountains
from the Lleyn.
'Here comes the sun,' he sings.
'There goes the sun,' I say.

1994
and Vivaldi's fine
though now and then I play
Hey Jude, Great,
wear a flowered tie.

*David Santer*

# FATE JUKEBOX

He's 54. His marriage
is quicksand. His job
and car graveyard bound.
But he was fresh enough
to be a Hamburg man
at the time of The
Beatles. he knew
the friend of a
needle-thin painter
who took bottles
and smokes backstage.
He threw up beer,
next to Stuart Sutcliffe.
He passed a comb
to John Lennon.
Then the fame zeppelin
took off. he was left
to plot his way
through a plain
German life. But
he'd shine in the
cellar nightclubs:
haystack hair, polka-
dot shirt; really
jerk his arms about.
Then he met Ursula
with the little boy face.
They came together,
like an A-side
and B-side,
thumb and plectrum,
bullet and gun.

*Peter Lane*

## LIFE STORY

He forced the world
to accept his weirdness
when what it wanted was
I Wanna Hold Your Hand.
But followed down every street, to every place,
he retreated. Then cleared
his throat, straightened
his tie, opened
the car door into *that* moment:
'Mr Lennon?' 'Yes

*Geoff Hattersley*

# NOWHERE MAN

A gargoyle springs to life
from an iron-faced Dakota rail,
pacing his time; patient
as a hunter in the grass
of Central Park, wild eyes
shaded by a trapper's hat.

Days of quiet stalking pass.
He is a feature of the street;
collects an autograph, his pen
scrawling the name he signs in,
lives by and through –
*John Lennon. December 8.*

He is the body politic:
a parliament of personality
and its lack convene
in his bone-domed chamber,
addressing the singular nation,
demanding warheads be armed,
the trigger held, caressed.

He flicks at the safety catch
as the limousine's door reveals
John: all cigarette and smiles,
a man who's found himself
thrust in and out of fame's
give and wrestle back.
Now father, lover, baker
before one of the holy four.

He is whippet lean, prints
Chapman as he passes,
securing a last negative:
calm in the camera's presence;
the most photographed of celebrities.

A combat stance – on his knees.
The reel snaps five times,

five bullets slice the projector's beam
as cordite stains the sky.
Hollow-point – assured
destruction: blood chokes out
the words he might have sung
and millions hummed, bought.

Eyes collapse. Heads fumble
for response. *It's such a drag.*
Satellites buzz, copy pastes
onto obituary columns.
The world reacts with the strum
of bedsit guitars and badly
affected accents, hallowing mimicry.

And some among us cannot cry;
they no longer have a mouth
to scream for them, and I
am thirteen, an ocean away,
waking to my radio alarm,
snoozing the full hour they play
tracks from the first albums
my stylus ever scratched,
dreaming through the imagery
of the hero against heroes
of the Love-Me Generation –
my one-and-only; my last.

*Damian Furniss*

## WHERE WERE YOU?

Where were you
the day John got shot?
What? Lennon!
Me, I was in Scotland, standing on a hill
a fool about some boy
     when I was younger
     so much younger
cried all night, maybe for him,
Radio Luxembourg whispered in my ear.
Imagine
being on a desert Island
with the Beatles
and 3 guitars,
a set of drums, what luxury
no need for records
and who'd want books
with blokes like that?
Heaven,
     there's no heaven.
It's my turn to be the walrus
goo goo
Imagine
ga-choo:
I'm so sorry
but there isn't room for you, too.
Imagine
they'd come on like a dream
and come together
walking hand in hand
my sweet lord
what a picture.

I wanna hold your hand
but you like different music
are on the dark side of the moon,
a whiter shade of
nostalgic reaction;
while I bop
8 days a week.

They're back in.
My kids think they're cool
know Here Comes The Sun
backwards
Sun The Comes Here
I feel old as the hills
that the fool has gone over.

Help me if you can
I'm feeling
a little help from
my friends, your friends
might be good
I am a walrus
goo goo
between Bowie
I am going Aladdin Insane
and Blondie
Call Me
I missed something
gently weep.

*Louise Hudson*

# EASY IF YOU TRY

*for my students in the Norton Creative Writing Class*

I was explaining to Muriel and Sheila and George and Milly
about how a poem can be split open by a detail in the right place
or just a fragrance floating in from what we might call real life.
I could tell they weren't having any of it, so set them off with a bit of a
  task.
*You're a piece of furniture whose language has no verbs. Write a*
  *love poem.*

Whilst they were scratching their heads a dream came back.
In the wood some men were dancing while others played drums.
They were chanting simple parts of a tongue without embarrassment.
My old French teacher, Ted Walton, so-called for the splendour of his
  quiff,
was hugging Fat Bob, a big bloke whose French trip a wise boy did
  not share.
His son David was slumped at the bottom of a tree, off his face.
Fat Bob had wired up the woods with speakers playing *Imagine* on a
  loop.
It was sending me out of my mind. It was his attempt to get us into
  poetry.
I wanted to burn Lennon, Ono, their fur coats and that piano and that
  house.
I still do. Fat Bob was never going to get me into poetry in a lifetime
and the day Lennon got shot it was all I could do to stop laughing.
I'm not really sorry even now. And the further away it gets the less it
  matters.

In my dream I whipped out a pen knife and started to carve in a tree:
*if we pretend hard enough the morning will come.*
I scribbled something down about it, a neat, clipped, side-of-the
  mouth job,
but Sheila and Muriel and George weren't impressed and quite right
  too.

*Mark Robinson*

# NEW YORK CITY BLUES

*for John Lennon*

*You do not cross the road*
*To step into immortality*
*An empty street is only the beginning*

The words will still flow through you
Even on this cold pavement,
Are heard in some far place
Remote from flowers or flash-bulbs.

In that city, on Gothic railings
Dark against the snowy park
Still a dead flower, a faded letter,
Already one month old.

'Life is what happens to you
When you're busy making other plans,'
This empty street
Is only the beginning.

Here, in your other city,
Riot vans prowl the December dark,
Remember angry embers of summer,
Familiar ghost guitars echo from stucco terraces.

Meanwhile, in the Valley of Indecision,
We rehearse stale words, store up unexpected songs,
Celebrate sad anniversaries.
Flowers and flash-bulbs. Cold pavements.

*You do not cross the road*
*To step into immortality*
*At the dark end of the street*
*Waits the inevitable stranger.*

*Adrian Henri*

## AND...

me and joey scott
and love me do
cost thruppence and biscuits
and love you too
and phil was paul
and i was john
and the girls
and the girls
and the girls were gone

and
we plucked penny lane
and we strummed old swan
and i was george
and phil was john
and me and joey scott
and love me do
was the only song
that we could do

and
a broken guitar
and sasparilla pop
and joey beat the biscuit tin
for ringo till he dropped
and phil did the love me do's
and i did the p-l-e-e-a-s-e
and the girls
and the girls
went weak at the knees

and...

*Paul Butler*

## LIVERPOOL ECHO

Pat Hodges kissed you once, although quite shy,
in sixty-two. Small crowds in Matthew Street
endure rain for the echo of a beat,
as if nostalgia means you did not die.

Inside phone-booths loveless ladies cry
on Merseyside. Their faces show defeat.
An ancient jukebox blares out Ain't She Sweet
in Liverpool, which cannot say goodbye.

Here everybody has an anecdote
of how they met you, were the best of mates.
The seagulls circle round a ferry-boat

out on the river, where it's getting late.
Like litter on the water, people float
outside the Cavern in the rain. And wait.

*Carol Ann Duffy*

## from **ANNUS MIRABILIS**

So life was never better than
In nineteen sixty-three
(Though just too late for me) —
Between the end of the *Chatterley* ban
And the Beatles' first LP.

*Philip Larkin*

# THINGS THEY SAID TODAY

TIM ALLEN knows all that stuff about the Beatles coming from Liverpool is nonsense. He was John's sidekick in the original Quarrymen in Portland, Dorset. So was his mate Dave. CHRIS BANKS knows different. Her dad owned a record shop in the Isle of Man. By the age of thirteen Chris knew both Don Lang and Jess Conrad. Then her dad got her the *Please Please Me* album. She'd always felt there was more to it than Cliff and the Beverley Sisters – 'Little Donkey' and 'Travellin' Light'. She swopped it later for a Black Sabbath LP. Told me in strictest confidence of course.

GARY BOSWELL, when little, felt the Beatles were Russian because he thought their hair was hats.

PHIL BOWEN's father Det. Sgt. Tommy Bowen was one of the two Liverpool police officers chosen to look after the lads on their visit to the Town Hall in 1964. Hence the autographs.

TIM BRADFORD felt a bit left out.

TOM BROWNING was born fourteen years after the Beatles split up. He first heard them in his dad's flat in South Wales around 1993. Remembers Lucy, the Blue album, Penny Lane.

PAUL BUTLER is one of the few Liverpudlians not to meet the Beatles. He nearly did though. His uncle Bob (whose brother was the Fourmost's drummer) invited him to 'meet some fellas in Beat Groups' – Fabs, Gerry, Cilla etc. – but Paul was playing football for the school! He now teaches at John Lennon's old one.

PETER CARPENTER remembers Wilfred Brambell's leer when he first saw *A Hard Day's Night* at the Epsom Odeon, and Shakespeare's (randomly mixed into the ending of 'I Am The Walrus') as two personal highlights.

TONY CHARLES says he never rated the Beatles much. Preferred the Stones. But he comes from Birmingham, so what does he know? And what's he doing in this book?

LINDA CHASE worked in a children's psychiatric hospital in San Francisco, and every single shift listened to the Beatles. Every single shift.

WENDY COPE had a kind friend who queued up and bought a copy of 'I Feel Fine' for her on the day it was issued. A few months later she ran off with her bloke.

JOHN CORNELIUS was in his early teens when 'Love Me Do' came out. Twenty-one when they packed up. Not all of their influence, he feels, was good. 'Fool On The Hill' describes his life best. He liked the Brazilian version.

PATRIC CUNNANE and his brother were reluctant to buy any Beatles' albums after Lennon's "bigger than Jesus" remark had enraged their father – a staunch Roman Catholic – so much, that if they did he said he'd break them over his knee.

MICHAEL CUNNINGHAM went to St. Edward's in Liverpool. Four members of his class took on the names of the Beatles, by which they demanded to be known from then on. This meant that someone whose real name was Paul became George and someone else Paul. Ringo's real name was Peter Stamper, who was also known as Frog. Surprisingly there was no-one in the class actually called Ringo.

ANDY DARLINGTON saw the Beatles at the Regal in Hull, 1964, in his Chelsea boots with Cuban heels. Also billed: Sounds Incorporated, the Rustics (Kenny Knight's second band), Tommy Quickly and Mary Wells. The Beatles were practically inaudible because of the hormone-propelled screaming girls hurling jellybabies. One threw an orange which hit George on the head. Chicks!

MIKE FERGUSON says that if you didn't have a crewcut hairstyle in Elk Horn, Iowa, in 1964 you would be called a 'faggot' or 'commie'. But he was only ten then, and had a shaved head, pledged allegiance to the flag daily, and dreamed through *Playboy* magazine. When the Beatles appeared on the Ed Sullivan show as hairy (and unlikely) iconoclasts, they changed most of this – at least the future haircut and pledges.

CAROL ANN DUFFY once wrote a play based on the Beatles performed at the Everyman Theatre in Liverpool. Somebody and the Dingles?

DAMIAN FURNISS has recently been burgled. They took the hi-fi and all the CDs. All the Dylan and all the Beatles. Bastards! But as he says: "the grooves are in the head and, after all, it's only Rock'n'Roll..."

JOHN GIBBENS remembers the Beatles coming round to his house for tea. They were just like they were in *A Hard Day's Night* – they kind of bounced in and went upstairs to his brother's room. They became like four older brothers in fact, sitting around playing the guitar, listening to Dylan.

ANN GRAY, like me, remembers the first time she heard 'Love Me Do'. That bit older though – hearing it meant Cliff didn't turn her on any longer – she went through Ringo then George before finally becoming John's.

GEMMA GREEN never saw a real live Beatle. The only ones she knew were trapped between album covers.

GEOFF HATTERSLEY lives in Barnsley, one of the Yorkshire towns Paul visited with his sheepdog Martha.

ADRIAN HENRI remembers John as a surly friend of Stuart Sutcliffe's initially. He was more than surprised then to find this transformed figure metamorphosed into a Rock and Roll star doing Chuck Berry and other covers after an investigative trip to the Cavern towards the end of 1961.

BRIAN HINTON is a character out of Iain Sinclair's latest novel, and knows what's the new Mary Jane.

LOUISE HUDSON doesn't. She also doesn't remember the sixties. So she must have been there.

DAVE IVESON's wife once danced with John in the Tower Ballroom, New Brighton. Since the lobotomy however, Dave has come to terms with this. So he says.

PAMELA JOHNSON remembers the 'People and Places' programme which was usually so grey and grainy. Then this group appeared and it was as if the world had gone colour! The harmonica and harmony undercut by the grittiness of Lennon's voice. It all seemed so radical then. But today... looking back...?

KENNY KNIGHT is widely regarded as the *actual* fifth Beatle. After disbanding his earliest group, the Ringo Vinyls – whose definitive first album *Yeah! Yeah! No!* has become "very collectable" – Kenny split for Hamburg where he was horrified to find Phil Bowen in a one-man show called *Yeah! Yeah! No!* Early hits include 'Ticket To Plymouth' and 'Being For The Benefit Of Mr Knight'.

PETER LANE's brother was painting Peter Lane's living room wall when I rang. "Tell me about the Beatles Ed," Peter asked later. "Oh, the Mopheads," Ed replied, "it was my heyday: I was playing sax, clarinet, bit of flute, I had my foot down on the motorway... I was talking about America..."

PHILIP LARKIN talked about his whole generation. The one before the Beatles.

GENISTA LEWES had a friend in Glasgow called Zita: 'Zita, Zita, meter maid, where would we be without you? Give us a wink and...'

LIZZY LISTER spent her early years entertaining Mr Kite in a barn on a Cornish farm, but could never get the donkey to waltz.

RUPERT LOYDELL isn't sure about all this really. I mean, they're over-rated, really, and of their time. And there's a lot of this kind of anthology about now, isn't there... "Phil, have you done those proofs yet?"

WENDY McBRIDE was sewing Peter's shadow back on for the umpteenth time back in 1962, when she heard guitars. Something to do with halos? Anyway, grabbing a bag of jellybabies she took off for Liverpool.

ROGER McGOUGH first saw John in action giving local DJ Bob Wooler a bit of a hiding at Paul's twenty-first in West Kirby.

LACHLAN MACKINNON was at school in Detroit when the Beatles appeared on bubblegum cards. He had never heard of them. Whoever they were, they added to the kudos of being British.

WES MAGEE was at a party in a Swansea cellar around the same time. Guttering candles cast dancers' shadows on the walls as 'I Wanna Hold Your Hand' spilled from the record player. All this, a golf shot's distance from the house where Dylan Thomas was born. Love and lyrics in the air as the shadows twist and shout.

LESLEY MARSHALL learnt to dance to 'She Loves You' on a huge, old handed-down Hacker, drifted away amongst the varying shades of yellow at the Beatles Exhibition centre in Liverpool and later told her children to sit down and watch *Yellow Submarine* as part of History... She could go on.

LLINORA MILNER used to wait for the noisy bits – (She loves you) YEAH, YEAH, YEAH! and OOOH! – but thought they couldn't be that great because her mum liked Tom Jones.

RUSSELL MILNER might never have known that a girl who pulled her knickers down was naughty if it hadn't been for the Beatles. And that the real revolution is in your head.

ADRIAN MITCHELL was the first person to write about the Beatles nationally. It was in a pop column he used to do for the *Daily Mail*. Appeared with Paul more recently, on the south-end leg of his last world tour.

ELMA MITCHELL liked them too. They seemed quite an innovation.

ELIZABETH MOORE's cousin once rescued her from this boring grown-up gathering by asking if she'd like to hear the Beatles' latest single. It was 'Yellow Submarine' – she was in awe – and it was absolutely true: they did seem to live in this magical parallel universe.

MIRIAM OBREY is moving into middle-age – has dead friends, partings, split ends, bridges and crowns; but less chance of being laid, having damaged lungs or hearing Mother Mary's words of wisdom sung as part of the National Curriculum.

WILLIAM OXLEY remembers a Beatle song coming from a mill in Middleton.

JEREMY REED was hit by the clothes first – high-heeled boots, black knitted ties, those tab shirts; the height of the shirts – then the music.

MARK ROBINSON owns no Beatles records.

JEREMY ROGERS does. His parents got him 'From Me To You' when he was eight. Met Lennon once on the steps of Huers Hut, Newquay in 1967. "Excuse me," he said, "can I have your autograph Jerry?" Has recently learnt to spell sherbet.

DAVID SANTER never thought the Beatles would make it. They didn't think he would either.

STUART SUTCLIFFE was one of the best painters to come out of Liverpool. He first came across John at art college in 1957. They became friends early 1959. He joined Johnny and the Moondogs on bass in January 1960, thought up their new name and died in Hamburg, a month before Brian Epstein secured the Parlophone contract, in April 1962.

SANDRA TAPPENDEN used to own a silk shirt exactly like the one Paul McCartney wore on the cover of *Q* magazine. She lives in Exeter. Paul doesn't. .

JAMES TURNER, a teenager at public school at the time of the Beatles' first LP, felt terribly out of things in those days. And minded. Now, he still feels just the same. But doesn't.

GORDON WARDMAN is the Wardman in Wardman and Watts.

ANTHONY WATTS is the Watts. Wardman and Watts: best rhythm section around.

GLYN WRIGHT was at school with one of the sons of the barber – 'selling photographs' – who, one fine day, whacked his brother in the face with a cricket bat. Complete accident of course. Seven stitches.